Fiddle Tunes ON Jazz Changes

To access audio visit:
www.halleonard.com/mylibrary

Enter Code
5384-3098-3824-0245

MATT GLASER

AND STUDENTS OF THE BERKLEE AMERICAN ROOTS MUSIC PROGRAM

Berklee Press

Editor in Chief: Jonathan Feist
Vice President of Online Learning and Continuing Education: Debbie Cavalier
Assistant Vice President of Operations for Berklee Media: Robert F. Green
Assistant Vice President of Marketing and Recruitment for Berklee Media: Mike King
Dean of Continuing Education: Carin Nuernberg
Editorial Assistants: Reilly Garrett, Emily Jones, Zoë Lustri
Assistant to Matt Glaser: Adrianna Ciccone
Cover Photo by Eric Gould
Author Photo: Nancy Adler
Cover by Small Mammoth Design

The fiddle tunes in this book were all written and performed by Matt Glaser with the following exceptions.
"After the Hair Is Gone," by Matt Glaser and Olivia Korkola
"Philip Grass," by Holland Raper
"Saints Alive!" by Serena Eades
"Walking in Jerusalem, Just Like Bud," by Chase Potter
"All the Soldiers" by Adrianna Ciccone

ISBN 978-0-87639-152-5

Study with

■ BERKLEE ONLINE

online.berklee.edu

1140 Boylston Street
Boston, MA 02215-3693 USA
(617) 747-2146

Visit Berklee Press Online at
www.berkleepress.com

DISTRIBUTED BY

HAL•LEONARD®
CORPORATION
7777 W. BLUEMOUND RD. P.O. BOX 13819
MILWAUKEE, WISCONSIN 53213

Visit Hal Leonard Online at
www.halleonard.com

Berklee Press, a publishing activity of Berklee College of Music, is a not-for-profit educational publisher.
Available proceeds from the sales of our products are contributed to the scholarship funds of the college.

CONTENTS

Introduction

Welcome to *Fiddle Tunes on Jazz Changes*. The title of this book may be perplexing to some, so let me begin by explaining the basic concept. Fiddle tunes are an incredibly deep reservoir of instrumental melodies that have been molded by the passage of time, and yet, they remain infinitely malleable. They are the native language for fiddlers, mandolin players, and guitar players in a variety of idioms. Moreover, fiddle tunes are generated from concise melodic cells. These melodic cells are memorable, and tell a musical story with just a few notes. Think of the opening phrases of "Turkey in the Straw" or "Arkansas Traveler," for example. In a short amount of time the powerful melodic motion creates indelible phrases that tell a story using tension and release. As the great composer Béla Bartók said, "Folk melodies are the embodiment of an artistic perfection of the highest order. In fact, they are models of the way in which a musical idea can be expressed with utmost perfection, in terms of brevity of form and simplicity of means."

I have been writing original fiddle tunes on jazz changes for a long time— at least since the mid 1970s. But recently, I began experimenting with taking phrases from famous fiddle tunes and paving them over the form and chord changes of jazz standards. Fiddle tunes (like bebop lines and Bach melodies) are predominantly flowing eighth notes. By manipulating the phrases of fiddle tunes to fit the underlying harmony of jazz standards, one develops a keen appreciation for good voice leading, as well as getting a lesson in "making the changes."

Many people learn to improvise on jazz standards through methods such as chord scales, where you learn a pool of appropriate notes to play on each chord. An approach like this might be valuable if you already play jazz at some level, and want to refine your skills, but chord scales do not teach you how to make up and vary a melody. By manipulating the powerful melodic cells inherent in fiddle tunes to accommodate the challenges of jazz harmony, you can create single lines that, like Bach's, embody harmonic motion, but are expressed in a purely melodic way.

The tunes in this folio fall into two basic categories. The first are tunes that use the melodies of pre-existing fiddle tunes, which are then manipulated to fit the form and changes of jazz standards. Among the fiddle tunes that you will hear quoted are "Turkey in the Straw," "Wheel Hoss," "Sailor's Hornpipe," "Liberty," "Soldier's Joy," "Fire on the Mountain," and others. Sometimes the fiddle tune is very obvious, and other times, it's quite hidden. (I might just use the melodic rhythm of the fiddle tune or I might just use the skeletal shape of the tune.) If you look carefully, you will find quotes from fiddle tunes throughout this book.

The second category includes tunes in which I created an original fiddle tune from scratch to go over the jazz changes. These tunes include no pre-existing fiddle tune melody. (Many of the ideas in this book are related to topics I address in *Bluegrass Fiddle and Beyond* [Berklee Press, 2010], and I urge you to get that book because the two volumes make a symbiotic pair.) To develop your skills as an improviser, it is most valuable for you to reduce the melody to its simplest sequence of pitches, what I call the "skeletal melody." Then, practice building back up from the skeleton and create variations of your own on each phrase.

The tunes in this book use harmonic progressions that are similar to those that occur in common jazz standards. You may see harmonic similarities to tunes such as "Sweet Sue," "Giant Steps," "Alone Together," "What Is This Thing Called Love," "I'll Remember April," "Guys and Dolls," "Fascinating Rhythm," "My Honey's Lovin' Arms," "All the Things You Are," "In Walked Bud," "Beautiful Love," and "Lulu's Back in Town." Many standards share similar harmonic and formal characteristics, and no tunes in this book are exact copies of any other tunes.

On the recordings, you will notice that I sometimes, in the heat of battle, play variations that depart slightly from the phrases notated in the book. This is just me trying to practice what I preach, and should not be a cause for alarm. As a matter of fact, the most valuable practicing you could do would be to make up variations of many of the two-bar phrases that occur throughout these tunes. "Theme and variations" is a common practice in western European classical music, and it is a concept that can serve the developing improviser very well. Instead of worrying too much about playing on chords, you can use your internal compositional ear to create manifold variations on a simple sequence of pitches. I suggest you try first to play rhythmic variations, and then attach pitches to your newfound rhythms. This will give your improvisations more vibrancy and life. Dizzy Gillespie was once asked how he approached improvising. He replied that he first thought of rhythms and then added notes to them.

The titles of some of the tunes in this book may seem obscure, but I'm a big fan of word play and riddles, and if you think about the titles long enough you might come up with some fruitful and otherwise hidden information. Similarly, the tunes themselves often contain musical jokes and riddles that I don't discuss in the text, but if you come upon any discoveries you would like to share with me, please feel free to write me at mglaser@berklee.edu.

To access this book's accompanying recordings, go to www.halleonard .com/mylibrary, and enter the code found on the first page of this book. This will grant you instant access to every example. Etudes with related audio are marked with an audio icon, generally a pair of tracks: one with the full band, and one without the melody, to serve as a backing track.

The American Roots Music Program at Berklee College of Music is a community of like-minded musicians interested in all kinds of early rural American music. Some of the students in this program have contributed their own original fiddle tunes on jazz changes, and those tunes appear at the end of the book.

The rhythm section on the recordings consists of three of my favorite musicians: Matt Munisteri on guitar, Sonny Barbato on accordion, and Dave Landoni on bass. I play fiddle on most of my tunes, and the following students from the American Roots Music Program play on the tunes that they wrote for this project: Adrianna Ciccone, Serena Eades, Chase Potter, Olivia Korkola, and Holland Raper, with additional help from Jenna Moynihan and Sumaia Jackson.

Most of the recorded tunes are played twice, and you will notice that on the second time through, I tend to vary the lines and improvise quite a bit. In general, these improvisations are not notated, but you can learn them if you wish, or just disregard them entirely!

1. Delicious Litigant

This is an original fiddle tune, based on a famous old song, that embeds the familiar melody in the matrix of flowing eighth notes. The repetitive nature of the A sections is balanced by a fair amount of convoluted movement at the bridge.

Audio 1: Full Track
Audio 2: Backing Track

Delicious Litigant

Matt Glaser

2. Back Home Again in Turkey

This etude uses the melodic cell from "Turkey in the Straw" and paves it over the chord changes of "Back Home Again in Indiana," a venerable standard that is played in traditional jazz circles, and has also given rise to various bebop and other modern jazz contrafacts, most notably "Donna Lee." Here, I tried to fully exploit the melody of "Turkey in the Straw" while accommodating it to the familiar harmony of "Indiana." The B section of "Turkey in the Straw" contains the important American rhythm known as the "cakewalk." (For more on this rhythm see the text to "Greta Garbo" p. 12 [etude 7])

Those of you who are skilled at musical forensics may notice the quote from Lester Young's solo on "Shoe Shine Boy" (from his first recording session), which occupies bars 11 and 12. This solo also contains the cakewalk rhythm. The second half of the tune beginning at bar 17 takes the melody up an octave, which leads us into the climactic moment at bar 21 in which I quote the fiddle tune "Limerock" on the A7 chord, as mandated by state and federal law. In bar 25, there is a brief quote from the Charlie Parker tune "Donna Lee," which occurs at the same point in the tune "Indiana." In bar 29, notice the "chromatic below, scale tone above" lick, which leads into a brief quote of "Sailor's Hornpipe," before landing on the ♭5 and mercifully ending this torturous experience!

Audio 3: Full Track
Audio 4: Backing Track

Back Home Again in Turkey

Matt Glaser

3. The Metaphysical Inquiry of Aged Joseph

This tune uses "Old Joe Clark" to reference a series of chord changes that similarly stress the ♭7 of the scale. As we have done in other tunes, I took the opening strain of the fiddle tune and modified it to fit over each two bars of harmonic territory. On the bridge, I introduce other familiar fiddle tune themes including "Wheel Hoss" for the first two bars, "Billy in the Lowground" for the next two bars, "Daley's Reel" for the third two-bar section, and finally "Fire on the Mountain" for its last two bars.

In choosing which fiddle tunes would fit over each harmonic area, I'm trying to follow the laws of good voice leading. I want one fiddle tune fragment to flow seamlessly into the beginning of the next. Keep that in mind as you make up your own fiddle tunes on jazz changes.

Audio 5: Full Track
Audio 6: Backing Track

The Metaphysical Inquiry of Aged Joseph

Matt Glaser

4. Just Gonna Be Me and You

The title of this tune comes from the punch line to a joke that some of you may know. (This is one of the two tunes in this book that use a joke's punch line as a tune title, the other being "Where's My Cookie?") Our approach to this fiddle tune does not quote any particular pre-existing melody, but instead embeds a strong, simple voice-led melody in a matrix of flowing eighth notes. This is a process I call "fiddlizing" a melody: take a song with a lyrical, vocal melody, and embed the most important tones in a torrent of flowing eighth notes. This is something you should try on a variety of songs! Our obligatory reference to "Turkey in the Straw" occurs in bars 12 and 13. Notice the extremely simple melodic mechanism used to get through the labyrinthine II V I progression on the bridge.

Audio 7: Full Track
Audio 8: Backing Track

Just Gonna Be Me and You

Matt Glaser

5. One Cufflink

The father of swing fiddling (and jazz humor) was the great violinist Joe Venuti. I was privileged to know Joe a little bit, and I once took a lesson from him. As I nervously played the song "Dinah," he hit my hand with his bow and shouted, "You're lost! You don't know where the [expletive] you are!"

Despite this traumatic experience, I have nothing but love in my heart for the great Joe Venuti. Joe was a good friend of the one-armed trumpet player Wingy Manone. As a prank, Joe once bought Wingy a gift of one cufflink, hence the title of this tune. "One Cufflink" uses melodic elements borrowed from the Kenny Baker tune "Baker's Breakdown." Be careful when shifting to third position in bar 13; I recommend that you make the shift on the E natural, which is the last eighth note of bar 17. I would then shift back to first position via the open E in bar 18. Towards the end of the tune you can hear brief references to "Wheel Hoss" as well as the R&B standard "One Mint Julep."

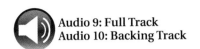
Audio 9: Full Track
Audio 10: Backing Track

One Cufflink

Matt Glaser

6. Where's My Cookie?

This tune (the title of which is a punch line to another joke) demonstrates how a diatonic fiddle tune melody sounds different when one varies the underlying chord changes. I have tried to find every possible chord substitution for the initial four bars, so that the same harmonic mechanism never repeats in the course of the tune. That gives us the following possible chord substitutions for the same basic idea. In bars 3 and 4, we have B7, E7, A7, and D7. In bar 9, we have F7, E7, Eb7, and D7. In bar 11, we have B7, Bb7, A7, and Ab7. And then, starting in bar 25, we flip the last two chord progressions. Notice how the same tonic-based melody sounds different in the light of each of these chord patterns. This is one way of sounding hip while letting others (i.e. the rhythm section) do the work. (Swing musicians call this process "forcing," while a more academic name for it is "harmonic generalization.") The most interesting bebop moment occurs in bars 23 and 24 with a classic #11 lick on the E7 chord leading to a nice altered phrase on the A7. In bar 29, notice that the melody is derived from a diminished scale, before ending with "shave and a haircut, two bits," because, why not?

Audio 11: Full Track
Audio 12: Backing Track

Where's My Cookie?

Matt Glaser

7. Greta Garbo

This tune uses a commonly occurring rhythmic motif in American popular music, sometimes called the "cakewalk" rhythm (or the *chalkline-walk* or *walk-around*). As discussed in "Back Home in Turkey" (p. 2 [etude 2]), the rhythm is eighth/quarter, eighth/quarter,

This rhythm can be found in the opening of "Turkey in the Straw," as well as in the opening strain of Bill Monroe's "Stoney Lonesome," which serves as the inspiration for our tune "Greta Garbo." Notice the slightly hidden reference to "Turkey in the Straw" in bars 14 and 15 and then again, obsessively, beginning in bar 19.

Audio 13: Full Track
Audio 14: Backing Track

Greta Garbo

Matt Glaser

8. Mr. Ed the Mnemonist

It may seem obvious, but one of the most important things you need to keep in mind when playing a tune is its form. How many bars long is it? Do you know where you are in the form of the tune at each moment? You should! (Because of the relatively long form of this tune, we only play through it once on the accompanying recording.) I use the melody of "Wheel Hoss" to pave my way through the shifting chords of this song, modifying the opening strain to fit the changes in harmony. Notice the similar melodic motion over contrasting chords. The initial strain moves from the tonic to the major seven and then resolves with the powerful melodic motion of 7 to 6. That takes place twice in the opening four bars. The same melodic motion takes place in the second four-bar section, but over a slightly different sequence of chord changes. When we get to the bridge I use the B section of "Wheel Hoss" to generate the melody. The only departure from "Wheel Hoss" is in bar 29, because every time any song goes to the key of E, I feel obliged to quote the melody of "Footprints in the Snow," and I do so here.

Audio 15: Full Track
Audio 16: Backing Track

Mr. Ed the Mnemonist

Matt Glaser

9. Motown Hot Dog

This tune does not employ any melodic motifs derived from pre-existing fiddle tunes. Instead, it merely fleshes out a melody similar to the theme song of a Broadway show tune that references "the largest floating crap game in New York." The title, "Motown Hot Dog," is a sly reference to the name of the leading character in this Broadway show. Good luck!

For this tune, we give you two versions. The first version is simpler and very close to the performance on the accompanying recording. The second version is more thoroughly "fiddlized" with constantly flowing eighth notes dressing up the skeletal melody.

Audio 17: Full Track
Audio 18: Backing Track

Motown Hot Dog

Matt Glaser

 Audio 18: Backing Track

Motown Hot Dog
Eighth Note Variation

Matt Glaser

10. Big Sailor Turkeywheel Liberty Polka

Here are two different tunes on one familiar set of chord changes.

The Terpsichore of Robert Wadlow

This was the first fiddle tune I wrote on a jazz chord progression. The changes are a famous harmonic labyrinth that function as a rite of passage for young jazz musicians. In the late 1970s, I lived in NYC and studied with the great jazz pedagogue, Adolph Sandole. Adolph had a small office in the Brill Building, New York City's famous rundown music business mecca. I wrote this tune as an assignment for Mr. Sandole, and I'm still tinkering with it after all these years. I wrote this tune thirty years ago, but it is too hard for me to play nowadays! I include the notation here because many people have expressed interest in it, but it is not included in the accompanying recordings.

 **Audio 20: Backing Track**

The Terpischore of Robert Wadlow

Matt Glaser

Big Sailor Turkeywheel Liberty Polka

The melody that I play on the recording is a recently composed polka that has many fewer notes than "The Terpsichore of Robert Wadlow" and is more melodic and lyrical, I hope. (You might notice references to the fiddle tunes "Sailor's Hornpipe," "Turkey in the Straw," "Wheel Hoss," and "Liberty" sprinkled liberally here, especially in the last eight bars.) I composed this tune by strumming the chords and trying to sing a melody that moved around as little as possible. Playing by ear and following the dictates of your internal melodic sense is always a good way to go. "The ear is the court of last appeal," as the great composer Paul Hindemith was purported to have said. The performance of this tune on the recording plays it twice. You'll notice that I varied the melody slightly each time. I consciously tried not to improvise on the chord changes, but instead to make up small rhythmic and melodic variations on each two-bar phrase.

You can play either one of these tunes along with the rhythm section track. Don't get discouraged with these chord changes; they are truly challenging! The way to simplify the harmony is by reducing all chord changes to either V or I. All the chords in this tune are either the tonic triads B, E♭, and G or the V chords that go along with those triads. So the entire harmony of this tune can be reduced to F♯7 going to B, B♭7 going to E♭, and D7 going to G. As I often say, all harmonic music in the universe can be reduced to either V or I. The most complicated chord changes in the world are either some kind of V chord or some kind of I chord. That being said, I've been working on these changes for nearly forty years, and I still find them to be difficult!

Audio 19: Full Track
Audio 20: Backing Track

Big Sailor Turkeywheel Liberty Polka

Matt Glaser

11. Road to Kansas City

You'll notice that almost all the tunes in this book are played with a swing feel. Recently, I've become obsessed with the feeling of swing in music. The feeling of swinging in music is a joyful, metaphysical experience. If you're lucky and work hard, you can master one thing in your life, and I want to master swing fiddle before I die! This tune is a swing version of a commonly played bluegrass fiddle tune. The rhythm section is playing a gospel-flavored reharmonization of the original chords, and the fiddle is playing a simple melody that is heavily swung. Pay special attention to the many syncopations as well as accents on the second and fourth quarter notes.

Audio 21: Full Track
Audio 22: Backing Track

Road to Kansas City

Matt Glaser

12. Lemon Shack Red

"Lemon Shack Red" is a fiddle tune based on the changes of "Limehouse Blues," which has a long and storied history in all eras of American music. I tried to use variants of the same melodic cell over the four bars of C7 as well of the four bars of A7. Other than that, I tried to make up long eighth-note lines that cover the full range of the fiddle in first position. Notice how, on many dominant seventh chords here, I made a point to hit the 3rd degree of the chord on a strong beat. This is the most important single thing you can do to demonstrate that you are aware of the chord changes. The 3rd degree of a chord is the most indispensable tone, because it is the one note that indicates the quality of the chord. If you can accurately hit the 3rd degree of the chord on a strong beat, you have definitely "made the changes."

A "triplet advisory" has been issued for the last few bars of this tune. Although these triplets may seem technically challenging, notice how the 7, 5, or 3 of a chord lands decisively on a strong beat.

Audio 23: Full Track
Audio 24: Backing Track

Lemon Shack Red

Matt Glaser

13. After the Hair Is Gone

This is a mash-up of the fiddle tune "Red Haired Boy" and the venerable jazz standard "After You've Gone." I am proud to have been a co-author on this tune with Olivia Korkola, a fine fiddler and Berklee student. Olivia named this tune, and I believe it refers to the fact that I am completely bald. Compositionally, this tune uses a slightly different mechanism to conjoin its two parent melodies. You'll notice that the opening strain of "Red Haired Boy" sounds three times before the resolution phrase occurs. This allows us to pave our way through the sometimes challenging harmony of "After You've Gone." In bar 13, you'll notice a brief reference to "Little Rock Getaway," and of course, you should not be surprised to see an allusion to "Turkey in the Straw" beginning in bar 17.

The nature of the melody that Olivia and I wrote, combined with the relatively slow tempo compared to other tunes in the book, suggested a *strathspey* feel, which is a Scottish dance form. Jenna Moynihan, one of my favorite fiddlers on earth, is an expert at Scottish music, and she contributed the appropriate rhythms that would yield an authentic strathspey feel. She plays the tune on the recording.

Audio 25: Full Track
Audio 26: Backing Track

After the Hair Is Gone

Olivia Korkola
Matt Glaser

Audio 26: Backing Track

After the Hair Is Gone
Variation

Olivia Korkola
Matt Glaser

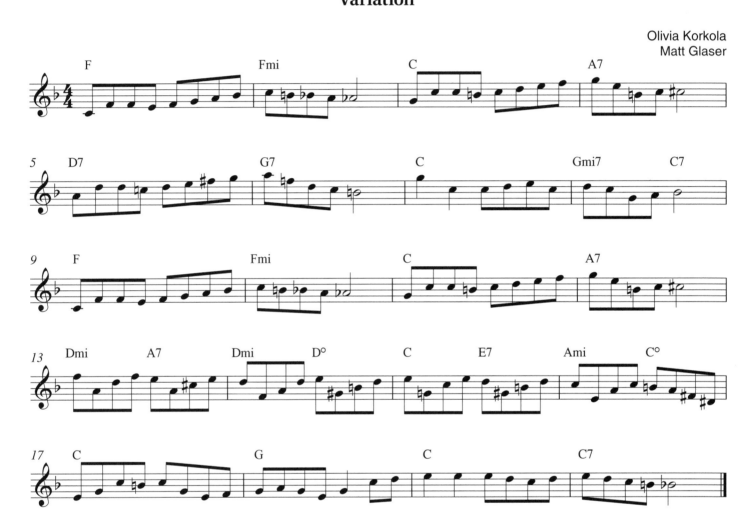

14. Saints Alive!

The original title of this tune was "Hagiography." The word "hagiography" means a biography of a saint, and the saints in question here are Saint Anne, Saint Louis, and Saint Thomas. Serena Eades, a fine Canadian fiddler, took the melody of "Saint Anne's Reel" and used it to create a new tune on the chords of "St. Louis Blues." See if you can find a brief reference to the melody of "Saint Thomas." In bar 15, Serena seems to have contracted the "Wheel Hoss" virus, for which there is no known cure.

Audio 27: Full Track
Audio 28: Backing Track

Saints Alive!

Serena Eades

15. Philip Grass

Wonderful Irish fiddler and Berklee student Holland Raper wrote this tune that we call "Philip Grass." The title is a play on words referring to the great contemporary minimalist composer Philip Glass as seen through the lens of bluegrass. The tune itself obsessively recycles a few little melodic cells and hopefully produces the same hypnotic effect that one associates with the award-winning music of Mr. Glass.

Audio 29: Full Track
Audio 30: Backing Track

Philip Grass

Holland Raper

 **Audio 28: Backing Track**

Philip Grass
Variation

Holland Raper

16. Walking in Jerusalem, Just Like Bud

Chase Potter is a spectacular young jazz violinist, multi-instrumentalist, and Berklee student. He went crazy and wrote a bunch of these fiddle tunes. I chose to include this one because it fervidly reuses one familiar fiddle tune on a melody that references to the great jazz pianist Bud Powell. This tune bounces back and forth between F minor and its relative major, Ab.

 Audio 31: Full Track
Audio 32: Backing Track

Walking in Jerusalem, Just Like Bud

Chase Potter

17. All the Soldiers

"All the Soldiers" uses the venerable fiddle tune "Soldier's Joy" as a basis for jazz explorations. The underlying harmony here should be familiar to most of you. Sometimes, I am playfully critical of Canadian fiddlers, but Adrianna Ciccone, the author of this tune, is a superb Canadian fiddler who has written a three-part harmonization for this tune. When playing three-part harmony on a fiddle tune written on jazz chords using all the guide-tone lines, don't forget to use taste, because you wouldn't want to overdo it! Get together with your fiddle playing friends and work up the three parts for fun, or just overdub yourself to see how they sound.

Audio 33: Full Track
Audio 34: Backing Track

All the Soldiers

Adrianna Ciccone

Audio 33: Full Track
Audio 34: Backing Track

All the Soldiers

Harmony

Adrianna Ciccone

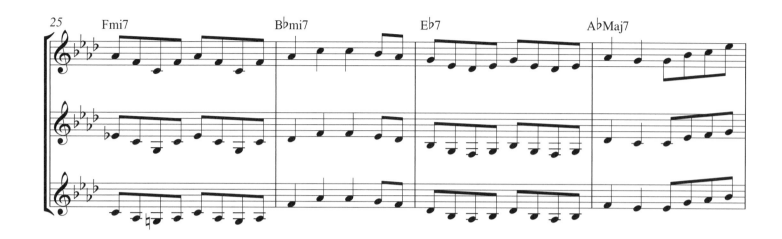

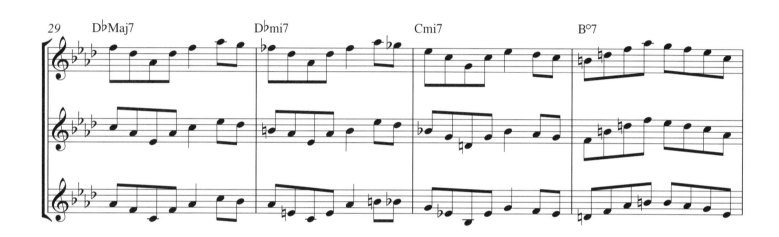

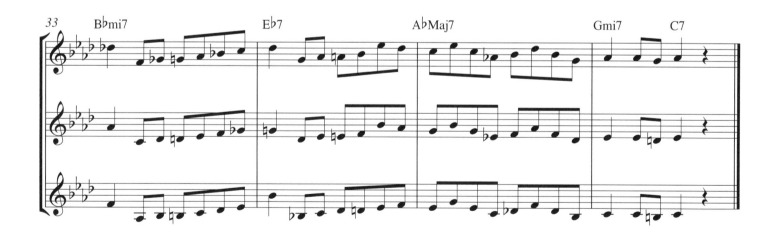

Conclusion

Well, there you have it. A whole bunch of fiddle tunes written on the form and changes of jazz standards. Enjoy playing the tunes as etudes and exercises, make sure to vary phrases frequently, and then try your hand at writing a fiddle tune of your own. Take a jazz standard that you're trying to master, and use a melodic motif from a commonly occurring fiddle tune. See if you can pave your way through the song, adhering to rules of good voice leading while "making the changes." Good luck, and let me know how it goes.

"Turkey in the Straw" forever!

About the Author

Photo by Nancy Adler

Matt Glaser is the artistic director of the American Roots Music Program at Berklee College of Music, and before that, had been chairman of the string department at Berklee for twenty-eight years. He is the only non-classical recipient of the prestigious American String Teachers' "Artist Teacher Award," an award that had previously been won by Isaac Stern, Yehudi Menuhin, Jascha Heifetz, Joseph Szigeti, and others. Matt is the first and only recipient of the Stéphane Grappelli Memorial Award, "In recognition of his significant contribution to the teaching and playing of improvised string music in America," presented by the American String Teachers Association with the National School Orchestra Association. He has performed widely in a variety of idioms ranging from jazz to bluegrass to early music.

Matt has published several books on contemporary violin styles, including *Bluegrass Fiddle and Beyond* and *Jazz Violin* (co-authored with the late Stéphane Grappelli). He has written for many newspapers and music magazines including the *Village Voice*, *Strings*, and *Acoustic Musician*. He has performed with Stéphane Grappelli, David Grisman, Lee Konitz, Bob Dylan, J. Geils, Leo Kottke, Joe Lovano, Charlie Haden, Michael Brecker, Kenny Werner, Alison Krauss, Béla Fleck, the Waverly Consort, Fiddle Fever, and most recently with Wayfaring Strangers—a band that fuses jazz and folk music. The *Boston Herald* called him "possibly America's most versatile violinist."

Matt served on the board of advisors of the Ken Burns' *Jazz* documentary, and appears in the film as a talking head. He serves on the board of directors of Chamber Music America and the American String Teachers Association.

Matt has performed at the White House and at Carnegie Hall with Yo-Yo Ma and Mark O'Connor as part of Stéphane Grappelli's eightieth birthday concert. He has taught at the Mark O'Connor Fiddle Camp, University of Miami, American String Teacher Association conferences, International Association of Jazz Educator conferences, and many others.